Altar Prayer Workbook

EARL ALBRECHT

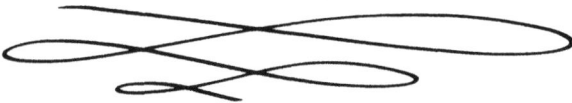

FOR USE WITH
COMMON (CONSENSUS), LUTHERAN,
AND
ROMAN CATHOLIC LECTIONARIES

SERIES A

C.S.S. Publishing Co., Inc.
Lima, Ohio

ALTAR PRAYER WORKBOOK — SERIES A

6841 / ISBN 0-89536-812-9   PRINTED IN U.S.A.

Editor's Preface

Here are altar prayers for every Sunday in the church year. Also included are prayers for Christmas Eve or Day; Ash Wednesday, Maundy Thursday, Good Friday, Easter Evening, Ascension Day (or Ascension Sunday), and All Saints' Day (or All Saints' Sunday). These prayers have been written with the needs and concerns of the worldwide Christian Church in mind. Based on the themes of the Gospel texts assigned to each Sunday, they reflect the themes from those readings.

Congregations using the Common (Consensus) Lectionary — United Methodist, Presbyterian, United Church of Christ, United Church of Canada, Disciples of Christ, Episcopal, Roman Catholic — will want to follow the designated Propers and their appointed calendar dates during the Pentecost (or "non-festival") half of the church year. Lutherans will want to follow the "after Pentecost" designations for that season.

This book is designed to lay flat on the pastor's (or prayer leader's) desk top, so that local or other specific prayer concerns may be pencilled in. It will then lay flat on the altar at prayer time during the worship service. A simple reminder will suffice to draw the congregation into a prayer response when the Prayer of the Day begins: invite them, following the leader's concluding phrase following each petition (*"**Lord, in your mercy,**"*) to respond with **"Hear our prayer."**

Advent 1

ALMIGHTY, ALL WISE GOD, creator of every second, minute, hour; companion in every circumstance. We praise you and prepare for your coming among us.

Lord, in your mercy, **R**/

Spirit of God, a new church year begins. The routine of daily life continues. We busy ourselves eating, drinking, living. We move through weeks, months, years, too busy to hear your Word. Fine tune us to the signal of your saving love.

Lord, in your mercy, **R**/

Lord of life, you are with us in the routine of daily work. Sometimes you penetrate our anxieties and preoccupations. You raise what is routine and give it new meaning.

Lord, in your mercy, **R**/

Son of man, equip us with your Spirit's power. Permeate our being so that we are always ready and eager for your coming. Replace fear and doubt with love and faith.

Lord, in your mercy, **R**/

Son of man, excitement for your coming increases. Target our excitement on that which is holy. Fill us with the wonder and mystery of your love. Thank you for our Savior, Jesus.

Lord, in your mercy, **R**/

[Local and other specific prayer concerns:]

These and all other prayers which you would have us offer, we now bring, Father, before your throne of grace. Amen

Advent 2

KING OF THE KINGDOM of heaven, fill us with desire
to do your road work. Cleanse our lives. Nourish us with
that food which produces fruitful repentance.

Lord, in your mercy, **R**/

Prepare us as a people of God:
 to be dissatisfied with past performance,
 to seek your will in service,
 to follow your guidance in serving,
 to be strong in the presence of doubt and frustration,
 to welcome and accept others as you welcome and
 accept us.

Lord, in your mercy, **R**/

Enable us to evidence changed lives:
 to do what is pleasing in your sight,
 to separate the dust and dirt of thought and
 deed from that which is pleasing to you,
 to praise you in word, work, and life.

Lord, in your mercy, **R**/

Holy Spirit, set our apathy ablaze. Set apart the pure
wheat of your intent. Work in all who govern our land,
the nations of the world, who control industry and com-
merce, education and entertainment. Support all who
lead and serve your body, the church.

Lord, in your mercy, **R**/

Advent 2

[Local and other specific prayer concerns:]

These and all other prayers which you would have us offer, we now bring, Father, before your throne of grace. Amen

Advent 3

GREAT GOD, you come to us new each day. We see and hear, yet do not understand. Praise you for your patient love.

Lord, in your mercy, **R/**

Loving Lord, we are assaulted by sights and sounds which must be questioned. We cannot believe or accept everything we see and hear. Help us discern your message and messengers from the insincere and untrue.

Lord, in your mercy, **R/**

Loving Lord, we are impressed by those who wear soft raiment, by those with charismatic personality and powerful presence. Forgive us, Lord.
> Open our eyes and ears. Grant genuine compassion for all who weep.
> Move our hands and feet to offer practical, caring assistance.

Speak your Good News through us.

Lord, in your mercy, **R/**

Loving Lord, you have prepared the way for us. We prepare for your coming again.
> Help us see the importance of self-sacrifice.
> Help us accept the challenge of change.
> Guide all who lead and serve in church and state.

May we never tire of justice work and peacemaking.

Lord, in your mercy, **R/**

Advent 3

[Local and other specific prayer concerns:]

These and all other prayers which you would have us offer, we now bring, Father, before your throne of grace. Amen

Advent 4

GOD WITH US, always, everywhere. We praise you for the love you reveal to us in Jesus, conceived by the Holy Spirit, born of Mary.

Lord, in your mercy, **R**/

Lord Jesus, grant us faith to live God-fearing lives. Restructure our faith. Influence us with the power of your living Spirit. Help us to be fearless and faithful in the presence of uncertainty.

Lord, in your mercy, **R**/

Spirit of God, motivate us to praise and worship you throughout each year. Enable your servants to proclaim your message with impact. Envelop your people that lives may be changed and charged with your Spirit.

Lord, in your mercy, **R**/

God with us, help us see your presence in the world around us, help us know your presence in our personal lives. You came into the world sharing the intimacy of a man and a woman. Prepare us for your unpredictable activity. Spare us from hasty action. Challenge us to faithfulness and fearlessness.

Lord, in your mercy, **R**/

Lord Jesus, God with us, you have saved your people from their sins. Your Word has been fulfilled. All honor and glory are yours, now and always.

*Lord, in your mercy, **R**/*

[Local and other specific prayer concerns:]

These and all other prayers which you would have us offer, we now bring, Father, before your throne of grace. Amen

Christmas Eve / Day

LORD GOD, demands and decrees are made which affect all citizens. We praise, worship, and serve you, our first allegiance. We are citizens of your kingdom on earth and in heaven.

Lord, in your mercy, **R**/

We thank you, Heavenly Father, for your Good News. Angels praised, shepherds told. Activate us for sacrificial service and joyful proclamation.
    Life has meaning.
    Trial is blessed with your presence.

Lord, in your mercy, **R**/

We pray for all who find Christmas a time of sadness and loneliness. Make known the needs of people in our community. Send us to listen, befriend, and encourage. Light our way out of one year into another.

Lord, in your mercy, **R**/

We pray for peace at home and throughout the world. Grant untiring conviction and unrestrained energy to all who work for peace. Help us see beyond the obstructions and differences, which divide, to the oneness we share in your forgiveness of sin. Glory to God in the highest. Grant us your peace.

Lord, in your mercy, **R**/

Christmas Eve/Day

[Local and other specific prayer concerns:]

These and all other prayers which you would have us offer, we now bring, Father, before your throne of grace. Amen

Christmas 1

WORD MADE FLESH, you live among us. Almighty God, you sent your Son because you loved the world so much. You are Emmanuel, God with us.

Lord, in your mercy, **R**/

God of good news, you are with us when the news is bad.
> Enable us to love those who persecute and violate.
> Enable us to forgive those who hate and destroy.
> Enable us to overcome every evil with the power of your love.

Lord, in your mercy, **R**/

God of Mary and Joseph, speak to all who have exchanged marriage vows:
> Reinforce all best intentions.
> Remove all destructive weaknesses.
> Replace selfishness and egotism with humility and love.

Guide us through all that is harmful; sustain us in our weariness, granting victory and peace.

Lord, in your mercy, **R**/

God of creation, support all caught in the uncertainty of dislocation. Guide leaders of every nation to a genuine concern for their people. Plant in each of us the desire to be our sister and brother's keeper. Grant sensitivity and compassion to serve in Jesus' name.

*Lord, in your mercy, **R**/*

[Local and other specific prayer concerns:]

These and all other prayers which you would have us offer, we now bring, Father, before your throne of grace. Amen

Holy Name of Jesus (C, L)
January 1

ALPHA AND OMEGA, Yahweh, the Great 'I am.' Put your name upon us and bless us. We praise and acclaim you, the only true God.

Lord, in your mercy, R/

Lord Jesus, child of Mary, named by angels, at your name every knee should bow. Word of God from the beginning, excite us with the name we bear,
    challenge us to be who we say we are,
    use us to set the name Christian before a skeptical world.

Lord, in your mercy, R/

Lord Jesus, what is in a name?
    We are not to take God's name in vain, but we do in many ways.
    Raise us above impatience and pride. Lift us out of self-pity and conceit to generous, outgoing love.

Lord, in your mercy, R/

Spirit of God, light our lives with your love, warm our hearts with your power, illuminate the name we bear, and share with the energy of Christ our Lord. We name Jesus Lord, Savior, Redeemer. Grant to all believers an undying desire to live the name of Christ.

Lord, in your mercy, R/

Holy Name of Jesus
January 1

[Local and other specific prayer concerns:]

These and all other prayers which you would have us offer, we now bring, Father, before your throne of grace. Amen

Christmas 2

WORD OF GOD, made flesh in Jesus, Emmanuel, our beautiful Savior. We sing for joy at your birth. All praise to the Father, Son, and Holy Spirit.

*Lord, in your mercy, **R**/*

Source of life, light to all, shine in our darkness:
    the darkness of doubt and despair,
    the darkness of failure and fear,
    the darkness of loneliness,
    the darkness of hopelessness.

*Lord, in your mercy, **R**/*

Enlighten us, Lord, to your presence.
Enable us to see you in the hungry and hurting.
Help us to recognize you in the rejected and destitute.
Grant awareness of your presence in unexpected places.
Welcome into our lives.

*Lord, in your mercy, **R**/*

God of grace and truth, move among your people.
    Make us militant peacemakers, shameless wit-
        nesses, sensitive servants.
Use the knowledge and faith gained from another year in the new year. Grant wisdom, courage, faith, hope, and love to all who govern. Grant the same, in abundance, to all their people.

*Lord, in your mercy, **R**/*

Christmas 2

[Local and other specific prayer concerns:]

These and all other prayers which you would have us offer, we now bring, Father, before your throne of grace. Amen

Epiphany
January 6

KING OF KINGS, Lord of lords, creator God, we worship and praise you. Lead us by your light through the darkness of the world.

*Lord, in your mercy, **R**/*

Star of north, south, east, and west, radiate your love throughout the world.
Lead your people in the way of peace.
Guide your people through adversity.
Uplift your people in the bondage of pain.
Shine through your people that the world will be set aglow with your love and peace.

*Lord, in your mercy, **R**/*

Child of Mary, Son of God, your entry into the world was disruptive. We pray for all who are persecuted around the world.
We pray for tyrants who tyrannize.
We pray for all who suffer.
We pray that faith, hope, and love will be victorious.

*Lord, in your mercy, **R**/*

Epiphany
January 6

Giver of every good gift, we bring you gifts of good intentions and earthly acquisitions. Remind us that all we have you give in trust. Forgive our unwilling stewardship. Cause giving to be a joy. We worship you with the gift of our lives.

Lord, in your mercy, **R/**

[Local and other specific prayer concerns:]

These and all other prayers which you would have us offer, we now bring, Father, before your throne of grace. Amen

Epiphany 1
Baptism of our Lord

GOD OF RIGHTEOUSNESS, author of baptism, Spirit of truth, all praise and glory, power and might are yours.

*Lord, in your mercy, **R**/*

Beloved Son of God, help us to know and do what is right. Hold before us the priceless treasure of baptism:
the life-giving power of your Word,
the sustaining, cleansing power of water,
the gift of new life and promise of eternal life.

*Lord, in your mercy, **R**/*

Jesus our Lord, servant, example:
hold before us the template of your example;
conform us to your humility;
sculpt us for your wise purpose.
Bless us to minister how and where you will. Enable us to mature in faith. Equip us for service.

*Lord, in your mercy, **R**/*

Praise you God, for peace wherever it exists.
Praise you God, for health, home, family, and friends.
You do not claim us by lottery, but by grace.
Praise you Father, Son, and Holy Spirit.

*Lord, in your mercy, **R**/*

Epiphany 1
Baptism of Our Lord

[Local and other specific prayer concerns:]

These and all other prayers which you would have us offer, we now bring, Father, before your throne of grace. Amen

Epiphany 2

GOD OF GRACE AND PEACE, we thank you for your goodness and mercy, for the Lamb of God to take away the sin of the world. All thanksgiving, praise, and glory are yours.

Lord, in your mercy, **R/**

Lamb of God, enrich our lives for service. You have taught us how to live, love, and pray:
 to love others as you have loved us,
 to love the least and lost,
 to pray for those who persecute, and who say
  untrue, unkind things about us.
Without your power and example all our efforts will fail.

Lord, in your mercy, **R/**

Teacher Jesus, we gather to listen and act;
 to worship you with hymns, prayers, and offerings;
 to worship you in daily work, studies, and leisure
  time.
You are always with us. Help us see life as opportunity to worship and praise you.

Lord, in your mercy, **R/**

Epiphany 2

Christ Jesus, energize your people for service. Move among the rulers of nations, guiding them in your way. Move among your people, cleansing and clarifying our goals. Be with the sick, weak, and despairing. Make us messengers of hope, advocates for justice, makers of peace.

Lord, in your mercy, **R/**

[Local and other specific prayer concerns:]

These and all other prayers which you would have us offer, we now bring, Father, before your throne of grace. Amen

Epiphany 3

ALMIGHTY GOD, creator of fish and creator of persons, all honor and glory are yours. We praise and thank you for the Gospel of the kingdom.

*Lord, in your mercy, **R**/*

O Lord, our Lord, your call to follow is communicated in many ways.
Other lords lure with promises of fame and fortune.
Laziness and lethargy entice us to do nothing.
Guide us through the mazes of ambition and uncertainty. Grant wisdom and the guidance of your Holy Spirit.

*Lord, in your mercy, **R**/*

O Lord, our God, steer us as a congregation, as a nation, as individuals. Empower us to work together as members of your body, the church. Aid us in learning and teaching, in giving and receiving, in listening and speaking. May all that we do be inspired by your Spirit.

*Lord, in your mercy, **R**/*

O Lord, our Lord, find us joyful, fearless followers. Grant patience and perseverance. Bless all who mourn the loss of a loved one, who are ill and discouraged. In all circumstances and at all times we pray to know your peace.

*Lord, in your mercy, **R**/*

Epiphany 3

[Local and other specific prayer concerns:]

These and all other prayers which you would have us offer, we now bring, Father, before your throne of grace. Amen.

Epiphany 4

GOD, OUR COMFORTER, source of all joy. You grant mercy to the merciful, comfort to all who mourn. We praise you, God of compassion and understanding.

*Lord, in your mercy, **R/***

Lord, we long to be rich in spirit and material things.
We avoid death and grief whenever possible.
Meekness is unpopular, poverty seen as failure.
We pity the dying and counsel the meek to overcome their meekness.

*Lord, in your mercy, **R/***

Lord, help us be merciful.
Help us to sincerely want peace.
Help us work for peace with enthusiastic determination.
Grant such a sense of purpose that we will not avoid ridicule and harassment because we speak your Word.

*Lord, in your mercy, **R/***

Lord, enable us to rejoice and be glad.
You are Lord. We serve you with our lives.
Guide your people to serve with genuine joy.
You have chosen the weak to shame the strong; the foolish to shame the wise.
We neither boast wisdom nor strength, but the Lord.

*Lord, in your mercy, **R/***

Epiphany 4

[Local and other specific prayer concerns:]

These and all other prayers which you would have us offer, we now bring, Father, before your throne of grace. Amen

Epiphany 5

GOD, OUR GLORY, Lord of all law, give light to our darkness that we may see and know your way.

Lord, in your mercy, **R**/

Lord Jesus, you label us salt of the earth. Many are on salt-free diets, live without you, reject you. Grant that saltiness which never loses its power or sense of purpose.

Lord, in your mercy, **R**/

Lord Jesus, you call us the light of the world. We are humbled. We laugh. We know the darkness of our thoughts, words, deeds. Charge us with your Spirit light. Energize us with your love.

Lord, in your mercy, **R**/

Lord Jesus, your expectations of us are great.
    May our righteousness be right
    our charity empty of self-interest,
    our praise truthful,
    our judgment charitable.
Guide leaders of church and state. Be with teachers and students. Sustain all involved in acts of mercy. May your presence bring strength to the sick and lonely.

Lord, in your mercy, **R**/

Epiphany 5

Lord Jesus, our light, salt, and hope, saturate our lives. Fill us with your Spirit. Grant creativity to find new ways to shed and share your light, to salt the world, to plant hope, and trust in your way.

Lord, in your mercy, **R/**

[Local and other specific prayer concerns:]

These and all other prayers which you would have us offer, we now bring, Father, before your throne of grace. Amen

Epiphany 6

RIGHTEOUS GOD, author of commandments, all praise and blessing are yours. Equip us for service.

Lord, in your mercy, **R/**

God of grace, grant strength where there is weakness,
   faith where there is doubt,
   love where there is hate.
Discourage us from being satisfied with anything less than your best.

Lord, in your mercy, **R/**

Lord Jesus, our brother, be guardian of our thoughts.
Grant patience that we not become easily angered,
   forgiveness that we not hold grudges,
      humility that we not expect more of others than we
         do of ourselves.
Replace criticism with compassion, self-righteousness with reconciliation. Lord, you forgive our sin. Enable us to forgive others as you forgive us.

Lord, in your mercy, **R/**

Loving Jesus, you love sinners but hate sin. Guide our guilt to repentance. Purify our intentions. Challenge our goals. Guide all in authority, that national and international leadership be led by your Spirit.

Lord, in your mercy, **R/**

Epiphany 6

[Local and other specific prayer concerns:]

These and all other prayers which you would have us offer, we now bring, Father, before your throne of grace. Amen

Epiphany 7

FATHER IN HEAVEN, creator God of covenant and commandment. You are Lord. We praise and thank you for your love.

Lord, in your mercy, **R**/

Jesus, Master, what you ask of us is difficult to accept. We are taught to be aggressive, to defend ourselves, and protect our rights. You ask us to be passive, submissive. Help us see the sense of your way. Grant us the wisdom of your love.

Lord, in your mercy, **R**/

Jesus, Master, we are taught to hate our enemy. We distrust those who are different, ridicule those we do not understand. Help us understand why we should love those who bother, betray, and ruin life for us. Help us see the wisdom of your will.

Lord, in your mercy, **R**/

Epiphany 7

Spirit of God, success comes to the just and unjust, also failure and adversity. Enable us to see the reality of life as neither reward nor punishment. Grant faith, hope, and trust necessary to work through life's trials and triumphs. Move within us to accomplish your perfection. Keep those in authority in your care. Guide your people to your perfect way.

Lord, in your mercy, **R/**

[Local and other specific prayer concerns:]

These and all other prayers which you would have us offer, we now bring, Father, before your throne of grace. Amen

Epiphany 8 *(Roman Catholic)*

GOD, OUR MASTER, made manifest in Jesus Christ. We praise you for your creation, example, and love for the world.

Lord, in your mercy, **R/**

Master Jesus, we pray your Spirit to strengthen us in life's anxious times.
 We enjoy happy times and the company of friends. We covet all that makes life easier and carefree. Help us enjoy health, home, and the life you give. Replace anxiety and regret with gratitude and trust.

Lord, in your mercy, **R/**

Master Jesus, guide us in your way. Plant wisdom in our hearts and minds. Place the desire for peace and reconciliation on the agenda of every world leader. Move people of abundance to gratitude and sharing. May your church proclaim your Word in attitude and action.

Lord, in your mercy, **R/**

Master Jesus, many try to be our master. Be master of all gathered here this day. Be master of the many organizations we represent. Motivate us to work together for your kingdom, in your name, to your glory.

Lord, in your mercy, **R/**

Epiphany 8 *Roman Catholic*

[Local and other specific prayer concerns:]

These and all other prayers which you would have us offer, we now bring, Father, before your throne of grace. Amen

Transfiguration of Our Lord
(Common, Lutheran)

GOD OF MOUNTAINS AND VALLEYS, we praise you for your constant love. All honor and glory are yours. You claim the Lord Jesus, your beloved Son.

Lord, in your mercy, **R/**

Lord, help us speak your Word in conversation and action.
> Help us appreciate your Word in the confusion of life.
> Help us live your Word through every temptation and opportunity.

Lord, in your mercy, **R/**

Lord, we hear your Word, but words are not enough. You are the Word made flesh. Give flesh to your Word in us:
> in service to others,
> in growth of understanding,
> in giving and sharing.

Lord, in your mercy, **R/**

Transfiguration of Our Lord
(Common, Lutheran)

Lord, go with us today. Guide us through the obstructions and intricacies of daily life.
Bless us: with the certainty of your love in time of confusion;
    with hope in time of despair;
    with trust in time of doubt;
    with love in time of anger.
We pray for all who try and fail. You are our loving Lord,
even when we fail.

Lord, in your mercy, **R/**

[Local and other specific prayer concerns:]

These and all other prayers which you would have us
offer, we now bring, Father, before your throne of grace.
Amen

Ash Wednesday

LORD, our gracious and merciful God. We praise you for every opportunity to know and experience your love.

*Lord, in your mercy, **R/***

Lord Jesus, the annointed, cleanse our thoughts, motives, actions. Remake our goals to be right and pure.
Rebuild our intentions on the bedrock of your Word.
Rehabilitate us to do what is right and good for right and good reasons.

*Lord, in your mercy, **R/***

Father, you know our intentions. Grant us the desire to do what is right and faith to accomplish it. Grant humility to turn from error and gratitude to be filled with thanksgiving.

*Lord, in your mercy, **R/***

Lord of life, plant a pleasant disposition within us.
Set us aglow with your love.
Fill us with the fire of your compassion.
Warm us with enthusiasm to serve you.

*Lord, in your mercy, **R/***

Spirit of God, forbid that we fast and pray for selfish reasons. So fill us with your truth and love that we will see doing and serving in Jesus' name as our reward.

*Lord, in your mercy, **R/***

Ash Wednesday

[Local and other specific prayer concerns:]

These and all other prayers which you would have us offer, we now bring, Father, before your throne of grace. Amen

Lent 1

LORD GOD, we praise you for your creation, freedom, and love. We praise you for knowing the tempter's power.

Lord, in your mercy, **R/**

Master over temptation, we applaud your victory. We pray for your strength.
Too often we are naive and gullible.
Too often we are weak and willing.
Too often we are proud and over-confident.

Lord, in your mercy, **R/**

Master Jesus we pray for the tempters of this world. May we not be numbered among those who cause others to do wrong. Change the hearts of all who use and abuse people. Plant in every criminal mind your will and way of love.

Lord, in your mercy, **R/**

Lord Jesus, be with all who are tempted to say, do, or think what is evil. Come to all who are tempted by fear and sickness, cruelty and pain, health and wealth, pride and power.

Lord, in your mercy, **R/**

May these days of Lent shed light on a dark world. May your Spirit move us to greater awareness and compassionate service. Replace the chill in life with your radiant love.

*Lord, in your mercy, **R**/*

[Local and other specific prayer concerns:]

These and all other prayers which you would have us offer, we now bring, Father, before your throne of grace. Amen

Lent 2

ALMIGHTY GOD, giver of every good gift, we praise you for the gift of your Son, for rebirth in the Spirit, for life eternal.

Lord, in your mercy, R/

Son of Man, lead us to worship in spirit and truth; clarify your intent, remove our hesitancy and uncertainty. Illumine our Lenten trail with your light. Sustain us with your life-giving water and an undying belief in your victory over sin, death, and the devil.

Lord, in your mercy, R/

Jesus, friend, encourage us to friendship with the misguided and confused. You personify God's love for the world. Replace our reticence and confusion with a kind boldness and mighty faith.

Lord, in your mercy, R/

Lord Jesus, in your name we pray for all who govern. May all authorities aspire to humble service and godly use of power and privilege. We pray for those at home and around the world.

Lord, in your mercy, R/

Lent 2

Almighty God, the world is your creation and object of your love. Sensitize us and every neighbor in this global village to your way of truth. Quench the thirst of ignorance with the water of your Word.

Lord, in your mercy, **R/**

[Local and other specific prayer concerns:]

These and all other prayers which you would have us offer, we now bring, Father, before your throne of grace. Amen

Lent 3

ALMIGHTY GOD, Master of the impossible, Lord of the improbable, sender of signs, forgiver of sins. We worship and praise you.

Lord, in your mercy, **R/**

Son of Man, Savior of the world. Grant us courage to take risks. Grant us wisdom to realize our foolishness and know your will, to not equate failure with error or ridicule with wrong.

Lord, in your mercy, **R/**

Friend of sinners, set before us your holy example. Man of faith, challenge us to greater faith. Lord incarnate, move us in the direction of your spirit and truth.

Lord, in your mercy, **R/**

On this Lenten journey we are led past the mystery of your miracles, the controversy of your associations, the pain of your prophecies. Fill us with joyful faith and hopeful trust.

Lord, in your mercy, **R/**

Lent 3

Lord, our Light, give light to our confusion. Help us know your Word in the face of competition and contradiction. Give light as we walk alone, in families, as people of God. Find us willing receptacles to relay your light. In Jesus' name we pray it.

Lord, in your mercy, **R/**

[Local and other specific prayer concerns:]

These and all other prayers which you would have us offer, we now bring, Father, before your throne of grace. Amen

Lent 4

CREATOR GOD, author of light and life. We praise you for the blessed gift of faith, for peace which passes all human understanding, for your grace.

Lord, in your mercy, R/

Son of man, remove the blinder of ignorance, all that compels us to be judgmental, desire what is foolish, covet, reject what is good.

Lord, in your mercy, R/

Jesus, Lord and servant, guide us in your way. Enable us to recognize our sin. Enable us —
    To want what you want for us.
    To ask for what you give to us.
    To give thanks for all we receive.
Praise you, our righteous judge.

Lord, in your mercy, R/

Jesus, our deliverer. Praise you for your patience, wisdom, and forgiveness. Guide the attitudes and actions of all who govern and who are governed. Combine mercy and might, leadership and love, power and praise of you.

Lord, in your mercy, R/

Lent 4

Father, Son, and Holy Spirit, make our Lenten journey one of increasing faith and personal commitment.
Grant faith and strength to bear the burdens of each
day. May our lives give credence to our beliefs.

Lord, in your mercy, **R/**

[Local and other specific prayer concerns:]

These and all other prayers which you would have us
offer, we now bring, Father, before your throne of grace.
Amen

Lent 5

GOD OF COMPASSION, we thank you for prayers answered, blessings received, sins forgiven. We praise you for the priceless gift of faith, the illuminating light of your Word for life.

Lord, in your mercy, **R/**

Lord, the resurrection, we bring before you those known to us who are seriously ill in body and spirit . . . people who are troubled by the demands of living . . . people who fear growing old . . . all who suffer the consequences of foolish decisions . . . all who lack adequate food and shelter. Lord, use us to accomplish your work in your name.

Lord, in your mercy, **R/**

Lord, the life, come with us to live your life. Be with families, communities, congregations, nations. We dedicate ourselves to do your work. Help us take time to pray and grant faith to believe that prayers are heard.

Lord, in your mercy, **R/**

Lent 5

Lord, move us to give of ourselves:
   to forgive the unforgiving,
   to shower the sullen and miserable with kindness.
Direct and protect every leader. Grant wisdom to every electorate. Make us exemplary servants of Christ Jesus in word and deed.

Lord, in your mercy, **R/**

[Local and other specific prayer concerns:]

These and all other prayers which you would have us offer, we now bring, Father, before your throne of grace. Amen

Lent 6
Passion Sunday

GOD OF GOLGOTHA, praise you for your goodness and mercy, love and grace. We hail you, King.

Lord, in your mercy, **R**/

King of the Jews, you asked your disciples to watch and pray that they not enter into temptation. Enable us, Lord, to watch with wisdom, pray with conviction, trust with certainty.

Lord, in your mercy, **R**/

Blood of the covenant, empower our prayers, cleanse our lives. Grant wisdom to see the danger of false choices, the treachery of the deceitful tempter, the reality of our weakness ard gullibility.

Lord, in your mercy, **R**/

King of kings, lay before us the responsibility of affluence, the temptation to pervert power. Rule the lives of all who rule. Save us from ourselves. Master us with the potency of your love.

Lord, in your mercy, **R**/

Lent 6
Passion Sunday

Son of God, Savior of criminal and innocent. Give strength to the weak, hope to the discouraged. We rejoice in the newness of spring, the resurrection power of God, the forgiveness of sin.

Lord, in your mercy, **R**/

[Local and other specific prayer concerns:]

These and all other prayers which you would have us offer, we now bring, Father, before your throne of grace. Amen

Lent 6
Palm Sunday

GOD OF MOUNTAIN, COLT, AND BRANCH, the universe expresses your majesty. Hosanna to the Son of David.

Lord, in your mercy, **R**/

Prophet Jesus, find us willing workers in your kingdom — going where you ask, doing what you ask. May anonymity not disappoint, nor fear discourage, but commitment prod us to service.

Lord, in your mercy, **R**/

Son of David, you chose the lowly way. We are often impressed by extravagance, excited by pomp and pageantry. Cleanse our attitudes. People praised and applauded you without understanding who you are. Forgive our lack of understanding. Lead us to your truth.

Lord, in your mercy, **R**/

Lent 6
Palm Sunday

Humble Lord, King on a colt, your cross waits.
    Praise you for your example.
    Praise you for your patient love.
    Praise you for your faithful forgiveness.
    Praise you for your hope and grace.
We applaud you, Lord, and dedicate our lives to you.
Make your way our way, your Word our word, your will
our will. In Jesus' name we pray it.

Lord, in your mercy, **R**/

[Local and other specific prayer concerns:]

These and all other prayers which you would have us
offer, we now bring, Father, before your throne of grace.
Amen

Maundy Thursday

ALMIGHTY GOD OF WORD AND WATER, glory, power, and might belong to you. Praise you for your exemplary love.

Lord, in your mercy, R/

Lord Jesus, you willingly laid aside your garments to wash your disciples' feet. Help us lay aside those things which inhibit us from serving.

Lord, in your mercy, R/

Lord Jesus, you met resistance among your own. With loving persistence you accomplished your task. Help us understand your will; grant commitment to fulfill it.

Lord, in your mercy, R/

Jesus, Lord, you place before us a new commandment: to love one another even as you have loved us. Enable us to see and accept the cross in love. Make us strong in faith to love and care as you do.

Lord, in your mercy, R/

Maundy Thursday

Lord of towel, table, neighbor, and life. Guide our lives, cleanse our prayers, bring peace, hope, and strength to all who are sick. Grant humility to the proud and your loving friendship to all who are lonely and upset. Wash us for daily service.

Lord, in your mercy, R/

[Local and other specific prayer concerns:]

These and all other prayers which you would have us offer, we now bring, Father, before your throne of grace. Amen

Good Friday

Leader: advise the worshipers their response will be "We claim you Lord."

GOD OF GARDEN SPLENDOR, gardens are our downfall. We choose the forbidden fruit and fall asleep in them. We praise creation and ignore the creator. We turn your creation into a curse.
Jesus of Nazareth, King of the Jews.

We claim you Lord.

Witness to truth, shed light on the truth about ourselves. Replace every wish for revenge with the desire for pardon and reconciliation.
Jesus of Nazareth, King of the Jews.

We claim you Lord.

Lord, raise every claim of discipleship to the level of sacrificial service. Wipe denial from our lips and hypocrisy from our actions.
Jesus of Nazareth, King of the Jews.

We claim you Lord.

Lord, life is filled with options and preferences. Barabbas symbolizes every foolish choice and unwise act. Grant us the ability to know your will.
Jesus of Nazareth, King of the Jews.

We claim you Lord.

Good Friday

Leader: advise the worshipers their response will be "We claim you Lord."

Jesus of Nazareth, ridiculed as king of the Jews, we claim you Lord. We have no king but Jesus. Your saving work is finished. We recall your suffering love. You are Emmanuel — God with us. You live and we give thanks.

Jesus of Nazareth, King of the Jews.

We claim you Lord.

[Local and other specific prayer concerns:]

These and all other prayers which you would have us offer, we now bring, Father, before your throne of grace. Amen

Easter Day

ALMIGHTY GOD, we praise you for raising Christ Jesus from the dead. Because he lives, we shall live also. We praise you for your love and peace which goes beyond all human understanding.

Lord, in your mercy, **R**/

Risen Lord Jesus, we praise you for your forgiveness of sin. We praise you for the freedom we know in you and the fellowship we enjoy in your name.

Lord, in your mercy, **R**/

Risen Lord Jesus, you lived your life for others, gave your life for others. Spare us from turning your gift of faith into selfish spiritual pride. Help us move among all your people, in your name and with your love.

Lord, in your mercy, **R**/

Risen Lord Jesus, we pray for all who do not yet know you. We pray for all who are troubled by doubt and fear. We pray for all who have turned over their life to you. Grant your light, life, and love to shine on them in abundance.

Lord, in your mercy, **R**/

Easter Day

Christ the Lord is risen indeed. All praise to you, Almighty God. All honor and glory are yours, now and forever.

*Lord, in your mercy, **R**/*

[Local and other specific prayer concerns:]

These and all other prayers which you would have us offer, we now bring, Father, before your throne of grace. Amen

Easter 2

ALMIGHTY GOD, author of peace. We thank and praise you for that peace which is beyond all understanding. We thank you for the Prince of Peace.

Lord, in your mercy, **R/**

Your peace be with us, Lord, to overcome troubled, fearful, doubting lives. Our pestering for proof reveals our torpid faith. Bless us with your peace.

Lord, in your mercy, **R/**

Your peace be with us, Lord, to keep us strong in faith when unable to see or touch. We panic, look for answers, cry out in fear. You are with us. Implant your peace in us that we will be able to share it with others.

Lord, in your mercy, **R/**

Peace of God, work your signs in every hurting life. We remember those who mourn the loss of loved ones . . . who agonize over a hospitalized friend . . . who suffer today and dread tomorrow . . .

Lord, in your mercy, **R/**

Prince of Peace, enable us to live enthusiastic lives, filled with faith and overflowing with love. May your will for us be accomplished and the name of Jesus glorified.

Lord, in your mercy, **R/**

Easter 2

[Local and other specific prayer concerns:]

These and all other prayers which you would have us
offer, we now bring, Father, before your throne of grace.
Amen

Easter 3

RESURRECTION POWER, we praise you for every prophet you send. So fill us with your Spirit that we will be powered to praise you in every circumstance.

Lord, in your mercy, **R**/

Lord Jesus, mighty in word and deed. Forgive our preoccupations. You are always with us. We are called to serve others in your name, to love others as you love us.

Lord, in your mercy, **R**/

Lord Jesus, you are Lord of all including the foolish and slow of heart.
Grant compassion to open eyes blinded by cynicism.
Grant hope to be optimistic in pessimistic surroundings.
Saturate every personality with your abundant love.

Lord, in your mercy, **R**/

Spirit of God, walk with us in daily life. Guide us as individuals, congregations, citizens of the world. You come to us in the breaking of bread. Move us to break bread in your name. Fill us with anticipation of your coming. Protect all who serve in church and state. Open our eyes, trigger our motivations to do your kingdom work.

Lord, in your mercy, **R**/

Easter 3

[Local and other specific prayer concerns:]

These and all other prayers which you would have us offer, we now bring, Father, before your throne of grace. Amen

Easter 4

SHEPHERD GOD OF THE ABUNDANT LIFE, we praise you for your continuous concern. You are the Way, the Truth, and the Life.

Lord, in your mercy, **R/**

Shepherd Guardian, dissuade us from tempting short-cuts and devious conduct. Your way of truth requires travel on the narrow way, through the needle eye of your grace.

Lord, in your mercy, **R/**

Good Shepherd, other shepherds entice. Offers of success, security, and salvation attract us. Lead us past every seduction. Enable us to hear and heed your guidance.

Lord, in your mercy, **R/**

Door of the Kingdom, you died for all, welcome all.
   Remove the restrictions we create.
   Destroy barriers of prejudice and bigotry.
   Cause conceit to crumble and self-righteousness to
       atrophy.
   Rebuild our lives with tolerance, acceptance for
       others, and love for neighbor.

Lord, in your mercy, **R/**

Lord, fill us with joyful resurrection news. Take us to
the rejected neighbor, lonely sister, angry brother, and
move us to do your will in Jesus' name.

*Lord, in your mercy, **R**/*

[Local and other specific prayer concerns:]

These and all other prayers which you would have us
offer, we now bring, Father, before your throne of grace.
Amen

Easter 5

ALMIGHTY GOD, provider, caring counselor, we praise you for sending the Way, the Truth, and the Life into the world. We praise you for making yourself known in Jesus.

Lord, in your mercy, **R/**

Lord Jesus, heavenly housekeeper, you have prepared a place for us. We praise you for your loving foresight.
You welcome us despite our callous conduct.
You love us despite our hateful behavior.
You are compassionate and we egocentered.

Lord, in your mercy, **R/**

Lord Jesus, we believe that you and the Father are one. We do not understand, yet believe. We love you, risen Lord. Make our faith real and practical.
Enable others to know you through us.
Enable us to know you through others.

Lord, in your mercy, **R/**

Lord Jesus, our comfort. By your power we are strengthened to face the troubles of life. Grant your powerful peace to the distressed and depressed. Empower us to accomplish your greater works in your name.

Lord, in your mercy, **R/**

Easter 5

[Local and other specific prayer concerns:]

These and all other prayers which you would have us offer, we now bring, Father, before your throne of grace. Amen

Easter 6

ALMIGHTY GOD OF LOVE, in whom we live, move, and have our being. We gather this day to express gratitude and praise of you.

Lord, in your mercy, **R**/

Jesus, Lord, help us keep your commandments in the routine of daily life.

Help us to accept the relevance of your commandments in this highly technological society.

Help us to acknowledge the importance of your commandments in these materialistic times.
Enable us to live our lives as a sincere expression of faith and love.

Lord, in your mercy, **R**/

Spirit of Truth, distract us from worldly ways. Motivate us to choose your best and only way. Fill our faith with vitality and our lives with joyful enthusiasm. Manifest yourself in us.

Lord, in your mercy, **R**/

Lord, our comfort and counsel. Be with leaders of church and state, with your people in need at home or in hospital. Be with those who know and love you. We especially pray for those who do not yet know you. Activate your Spirit growth in every life.

Lord, in your mercy, **R**/

Easter 6

[Local and other specific prayer concerns:]

These and all other prayers which you would have us offer, we now bring, Father, before your throne of grace. Amen

Ascension Day

ALMIGHTY GOD OF LAW AND PROPHET, Word and words, all honor and glory are yours.

Lord, in your mercy, **R/**

God of mystery and miracle, open our minds to your understanding. Replace questioning with faith, doubt with joy. Enable us to treasure the forgiveness of our sins. Enable us, each day, to repent of our sins.

Lord, in your mercy, **R/**

Lord Jesus, lead us on our journey through life, day by day, moment by moment. Bless us for each task. Speak your Word of love. Help us carry your light burden. Clothe us with power from on high.

Lord, in your mercy, **R/**

Lord Jesus, you lay your kingdom work upon us. You entrust us with disciple-making and baptizing. Guide us in every effort that we work with sincerity and love, that the Father, Son, and Holy Spirit may be glorified.

Lord, in your mercy, **R/**

Ascension Day

Faithful Lord, bring peace to our time. Make us instruments for your peace. May the leaders of every nation be faithful to your will. May we be faithful to our leaders. Work in us and through us.

*Lord, in your mercy, **R/***

[Local and other specific prayer concerns:]

These and all other prayers which you would have us offer, we now bring, Father, before your throne of grace. Amen

Easter 7

ALMIGHTY GOD, creator, sustainer, Word made flesh, we praise you.

*Lord, in your mercy, **R**/*

Only true God, you entrust to all believers the task of making your will and way known.
    May insincerity not cloud your good news.
    May hypocrisy not invalidate your Word.
    May actions not contradict what is said.

*Lord, in your mercy, **R**/*

Holy Father, you created us to be individuals in your image. Help us celebrate our individuality. You bless us with different gifts, talents, and opportunities. Fill us with gratitude for the variety of expression and novelty of service. You love each person of your creation, a child of your grace.

*Lord, in your mercy, **R**/*

Spirit of the living God, only through your powerful presence can oneness be accomplished. Rule the hearts and minds of leaders of church and state. Bother us with your Word. Reinforce us with your love. Fill us with joy and hope in your promised Word.

*Lord, in your mercy, **R**/*

Easter 7

[Local and other specific prayer concerns:]

These and all other prayers which you would have us offer, we now bring, Father, before your throne of grace. Amen

The Day of Pentecost

ALMIGHTY GOD AND LORD, we praise you for your love and compassion. We praise you for your Holy Spirit.

> *Peace be with you.*
> **Amen, Lord Jesus.**

Holy Spirit of the living God. You are always with us. You call us to love and not to judge. Fill us with good ambitions. Motivate us to worthy activity.

> *Peace be with you.*
> **Amen, Lord Jesus.**

We thank you, Lord, for every place on earth where people are free to gather and worship you. We thank you, Lord, for people to whom this is a priceless gift.

> *Peace be with you.*
> **Amen, Lord Jesus.**

We thank you, Lord, for every blessing: justice, freedom, health, education, and faith. Forgive us when we take these for granted. You send us to share these gifts with others in your name.

> *Peace be with you.*
> **Amen, Lord Jesus.**

The Day of Pentecost

Breathe your Holy Spirit on each of us. Fill us with the gifts of the Spirit. Enable us to accomplish your will in a wanting world.

> *Peace be with you.*
> **Amen, Lord Jesus.**

Lord, we receive your Holy Spirit as we are able. Grant us faith, hope, and love equal to each day's demands.

> *Peace be with you.*
> **Amen, Lord Jesus.**

[Local and other specific prayer concerns:]

These and all other prayers which you would have us offer, we now bring, Father, before your throne of grace. Amen

Trinity Sunday

GOD OF GRACE, God of love, we praise you for making us partners in the fellowship of life.

Lord, in your mercy, **R**/

Almighty God, the only true authority, you instruct us to go, make disciples of all nations. You ask that we not merely be disciples, but go and do the work of a disciple.

Lord, in your mercy, **R**/

Holy Spirit, you work in us through the fellowship of community and congregation. You welcome all people from all places. May your Spirit, working in us, make us sincere welcomers.

Lord, in your mercy, **R**/

Lord Jesus, only Son from the Father. We praise you for your patient love. Even at the Galilean mountain some disciples doubted you. Forgive us when we doubt. Move us from doubt to conviction.

Lord, in your mercy, **R**/

God the Father, God the Son, God the Holy Spirit, one God. You come to us. You work in us and through us. Work your will and accomplish your purpose.

Lord, in your mercy, **R**/

Trinity Sunday

[Local and other specific prayer concerns:]

These and all other prayers which you would have us offer, we now bring, Father, before your throne of grace. Amen

Proper 4 — May 29-June 4 *(Common)*
Pentecost 2 *(Lutheran)*
Ordinary Time 9 *(Roman Catholic)*

RIGHTEOUS GOD, creator, sustainer. You spoke and your will was accomplished. We praise you for your Word, Jesus Christ.

Lord, in your mercy, **R/**

Lord. Lord. How easy it is to speak your name. How easy it is to be busy with superficial activity. How tempting it is to feel that you are indebted to us.

Lord, in your mercy, **R/**

Lord, help us choose that solid rock of faith, and trust your saving grace. Help us acknowledge your gift of forgiveness, not earned, but endowed. Enable us to withstand the destructive forces of life.

Lord, in your mercy, **R/**

Lord, help us reach out to those who make self-destructive choices. Well up in us a genuine concern for those who suffer from inadequate and unwise preparation. Forgive our faithlessness and foolishness.

Lord, in your mercy, **R/**

Proper 4 — May 29-June 4 *(Common)*
Pentecost 2 *(Lutheran)*
Ordinary Time 9 *(Roman Catholic)*

[Local and other specific prayer concerns:]

These and all other prayers which you would have us offer, we now bring, Father, before your throne of grace. Amen

Corpus Christi *(Roman Catholic)*

ALMIGHTY GOD, living Father, Creator, we praise you for your wisdom, power, and love.

Lord, in your mercy, **R/**

Living bread, live in us, sustain us for the demands of daily life and the promised eternal life. Fill us with spiritual nutrient.

Lord, in your mercy, **R/**

Son of man, you place before us the banquet of your body and blood. Fill us with the nourishment of your real food and drink.

Lord, in your mercy, **R/**

Lord, our Truth, you feed us for service. We are fueled for your kingdom work — charged with the energy of your compassion — triggered by the example of your humble service. The poor, impoverished, abused, and forgotten wait for us to share the banquet table.

Lord, in your mercy, **R/**

Ever present Lord, you nourish and satisfy us. With thankful hearts we are equipped for ministry. May you find your people willing workers. May we, part of your body in the world, play a part in accomplishing your will.

Lord, in your mercy, **R/**

Corpus Christi *(Roman Catholic)*

[Local and other specific prayer concerns:]

These and all other prayers which you would have us offer, we now bring, Father, before your throne of grace. Amen

Proper 5 — June 5-11 *(Common)*
Pentecost 3 *(Lutheran)*
Ordinary Time 10 *(Roman Catholic)*

GOD OF PROMISE, we praise you for your love of all people, especially sinners. We praise you for your mercy.

*Lord, in your mercy, **R**/*

Teacher, you challenge us to accept societies unacceptable.
You challenge us to forget self and to unselfishly befriend the repulsive and objectionable. Teacher, we need the power of your love.

*Lord, in your mercy, **R**/*

Teacher, you called Matthew. He rose and followed.
Replace self-interest with commitment to your will.
Replace personal ambition with openness to your Spirit call.
Fill us with mercy and mighty love.

*Lord, in your mercy, **R**/*

Proper 5 — June 5-11 *(Common)*
Pentecost 3 *(Lutheran)*
Ordinary Time 10 *(Roman Catholic)*

Teacher, in our communities live people whose life-styles are open to criticism. We quickly label them and those who associate with them.

Remove scales of conceit from our eyes.
Remove weights of callousness from our hearts.
Replace judgment with mercy.
Move us among your people with your power and
compassion.

Lord, in your mercy, **R/**

[Local and other specific prayer concerns:]

These and all other prayers which you would have us offer, we now bring, Father, before your throne of grace. Amen

86

Proper 6 — June 12-18 *(Common)*
Pentecost 4 *(Lutheran)*
Ordinary Time 11 *(Roman Catholic)*

RECONCILING GOD, we praise you for your creation work. You bless us with seasons, seedtime and sun-
shine. You are always with us. Blessed are you, creator
God.

Lord, in your mercy, **R/**

Shepherd Jesus, share with us your insight to better
understand the harassed and helpless, the empathy and
skill to serve. Help us realize our own needs. Bless us
with your love power.

Lord, in your mercy, **R/**

Spirit of God, drive out unclean spirits from every life.
Fill us with determination and perseverance to accom-
plish your will.
   Grant humility and courage, grounded in faith.

Lord, in your mercy, **R/**

Healer Lord, we pray for all who are sick, remembering before you those known to us . . . Grant patience
to all, filling them with joy and peace in your loving
presence.

Lord, in your mercy, **R/**

Proper 6 — June 12-18 *(Common)*
Pentecost 4 *(Lutheran)*
Ordinary Time 11 *(Roman Catholic)*

O Lord, the harvest is plentiful, but the laborers are few. Place us where you will, to do what you will.

Lord, in your mercy, **R/**

[Local and other specific prayer concerns:]

These and all other prayers which you would have us offer, we now bring, Father, before your throne of grace. Amen

Proper 7 — June 19-25 *(Common)*
Pentecost 5 *(Lutheran)*
Ordinary Time 12 *(Roman Catholic)*

GOD OF GRACE, victor over evil, creator of good. We gather to sing our praises, and to praise you with our lives.

Lord, in your mercy, **R/**

Jesus, Lord, teacher, you call us to teach and to follow. Place in our curriculum the word of your saving love. Place on the agenda of each day the desire to follow you in faith, the trust to follow you without fear.

Lord, in your mercy, **R/**

Jesus, Lord, servant, you show humility by the example of your life. You show joyful purpose in serving. Grant us the desire to be humble, caring, responsible people. Raise us to willing, enthusiastic service in your name and to your glory.

Lord, in your mercy, **R/**

Spirit of God, work your will through us. Guide leaders and people to a desire for peace.
Help us love you above all else.
Help us value your appraisal of your people.
May faith and love for you compel us to
acknowledge you before others.

Lord, in your mercy, **R/**

Proper 7 — June 19-25 *(Common)*
Pentecost 5 *(Lutheran)*
Ordinary Time 12 *(Roman Catholic)*

[Local and other specific prayer concerns:]

These and all other prayers which you would have us offer, we now bring, Father, before your throne of grace. Amen

Proper 8 — June 26-July 2 (Common)
Pentecost 6 (Lutheran)
Ordinary Time 13 (Roman Catholic)

GOD OF THAT PEACE which passes all human understanding. We praise you for every peacemaker in the world. We praise you for the peace you plant in our hearts.

Lord, in your mercy, **R/**

Lord Jesus, you challenge our selfishness.
    You challenge our priorities.
    You challenge our life view and lifestyle.
We are reluctant to hear your Word and to follow your way.

Lord, in your mercy, **R/**

Lord Jesus, you ask us to take our cross and follow you. Sometimes taking that cross makes us unpopular, causes division. But Lord, taking the cross also puts flesh on our faith, clothes fear with faith. Lord Jesus, grant your power.

Lord, in your mercy, **R/**

Lord, our host, you call us to be hospitable. In a busy, impersonal world, may the lives and homes of believers be an oasis of hope and joy. In an often uncaring and dishonest world, may all who name you Lord be ambassadors of love and peace.

Lord, in your mercy, **R/**

Proper 8 — June 26-July 2 *(Common)*
Pentecost 6 *(Lutheran)*
Ordinary Time 13 *(Roman Catholic)*

[Local and other specific prayer concerns:]

These and all other prayers which you would have us offer, we now bring, Father, before your throne of grace. Amen

Proper 9 — July 3-9 *(Common)*
Pentecost 7 *(Lutheran)*
Ordinary Time 14 *(Roman Catholic)*

LORD OF HEAVEN AND EARTH, we thank you for your mysteries and revelations. We praise you for your love, power, and peace.

> *Lord, in your mercy,* **R/**

Lord of yoke and every burden:
> forgive us for ignoring you, when we feel we have no one to turn to;
> forgive us for rejecting you, when we feel we must face life alone.

Fill us with trusting patience, sufficient for every circumstance.

> *Lord, in your mercy,* **R/**

Spirit of God, enable us to know the Father and the Son. Reveal your divine nature and purpose to us. Equip us with a gentle and lowly heart.

> *Lord, in your mercy,* **R/**

Son of God, reveal the Father to us and to a desperate world. Rule the life of every ruler.
> Subject every subject to your love command.
> Move among us, and within us, to move us to faith and all good works.

> *Lord, in your mercy,* **R/**

Proper 9 — July 3-9 *(Common)*
Pentecost 7 *(Lutheran)*
Ordinary Time 14 *(Roman Catholic)*

[Local and other specific prayer concerns:]

These and all other prayers which you would have us offer, we now bring, Father, before your throne of grace. Amen

Proper 10 — July 10-16 *(Common)*
Pentecost 8 *(Lutheran)*
Ordinary Time 15 *(Roman Catholic)*

CREATOR GOD of every season and every seed. We acknowledge your handiwork and power. All honor and glory are yours.

Lord, in your mercy, **R/**

Lord of life, we enjoy the peaceful quiet of your creation. Lord, forgive our irritability when that peace is interrupted. Enable us to use each moment to your glory.

Lord, in your mercy, **R/**

Lord of life, creator of senses; functioning eyes, ears, and minds are not enough. Grant sensitivity and insight. Sensitize us to know your purpose and will in all that we see and hear.

Lord, in your mercy, **R/**

Lord of life, you entrust the sowing of seed to us.
    Plant in us the determination to share your good
        news.
    Help us overcome discouragement and frustration.
    Fill us with love for the antagonistic, and those who
        oppose your Word.
    Fill us with the power of your purpose.

Lord, in your mercy, **R/**

Proper 10 — July 10-16 *(Common)*
Pentecost 8 *(Lutheran)*
Ordinary Time 15 *(Roman Catholic)*

Lord of life, we receive your Word with joy. May the cares of the world not undermine our faith and trust in you. We pray your comfort for the sick, elderly, and all with impaired senses. Power us to bring your love to all and to know your love in our lives.

Lord, in your mercy, **R/**

[Local and other specific prayer concerns:]

These and all other prayers which you would have us offer, we now bring, Father, before your throne of grace. Amen

Proper 11 — July 17-23 *(Common)*
Pentecost 9 *(Lutheran)*
Ordinary Time 16 *(Roman Catholic)*

ALMIGHTY GOD OF SEEDTIME AND HARVEST, of spring rain, summer sun, and autumn color, author of forgiveness and reconciliation, we gather to worship and praise you.

Lord, in your mercy, **R**/

Teacher Jesus, life is filled with puzzling, confusing situations. Good intentions and careful preparations sometimes reap discouraging results. Shield us from self-pity, disillusionment and cynicism. Grant your patient wisdom to each worker.

Lord, in your mercy, **R**/

Teacher Jesus, there seem to be more weed sowers than good seed sowers in life. We pray for all who disrupt and desecrate. We pray for all who attempt to confuse what is good and wholesome. We pray for all who introduce demonic alternatives.

Lord, in your mercy, **R**/

Proper 11 — July 17-23 (Common)
Pentecost 9 (Lutheran)
Ordinary Time 16 (Roman Catholic)

Teacher Jesus, grant us the wisdom of the sower.
   Grant us patience to wait for harvest time.
   Grant us a genuine concern for every weed flourish-
      ing in life.
You came to save sinners.
You challenge us to work among the weeds.
You challenge us to see the weed in ourselves.

Lord, in your mercy, **R/**

Teacher Jesus, you show us the best way. Fill us with desire to strive for your best way. May we experience the warmth of your forgiveness when we fail.

Lord, in your mercy, **R/**

[Local and other specific prayer concerns:]

These and all other prayers which you would have us offer, we now bring, Father, before your throne of grace. Amen

Proper 12 — July 24-30 *(Common)*
Pentecost 10 *(Lutheran)*
Ordinary Time 17 *(Roman Catholic)*

KING OF THE KINGDOM OF HEAVEN, we praise you for every treasure shared with us. We give thanks for the treasure of your love revealed through the Lord Jesus.

Lord, in your mercy, **R/**

Jesus, our trainer, enable us to discern treasure from trash. Motivate us to search for your Word without tiring, to sacrifice all to acquire it.

Lord, in your mercy, **R/**

Jesus, our trainer, hold before us the demands of treasure hunting, the relentless training schedule, the willingness to suffer pain and discomfort.

Place in our hearts the willingness to sacrifice other pleasures for your single purpose.

Grant us the vision of that single goal which makes other attractions meaningless.

Lord, in your mercy, **R/**

Jesus, our trainer, hold before us the inclusiveness of treasure hunting.

Spare us from allowing training to become a selfish ego trip.

Motivate us to encourage and assist others.

Open our eyes to the needs of the sick, lonely, abused, and rejected among us.

Lord, in your mercy, **R/**

Proper 12 — July 24-30 *(Common)*
Pentecost 10 *(Lutheran)*
Ordinary Time 17 *(Roman Catholic)*

[Local and other specific prayer concerns:]

These and all other prayers which you would have us offer, we now bring, Father, before your throne of grace. Amen

Proper 13 — July 31-August 6 *(Common)*
Pentecost 11 *(Lutheran)*
Ordinary Time 18 *(Roman Catholic)*

GOD, CREATOR, God of compassion and love. We praise you with our worship, and dedicate our lives to your will.

Lord, in your mercy, **R/**

Christ Jesus our Lord, we thank you for sharing your time with the thousands who followed you.
We consider our vacation time sacred.
We resist intrusion, are impatient with those who bother us.
Hold before us your example of compassion and caring.

Lord, in your mercy, **R/**

Christ Jesus our Lord, master of every situation. You care for every person. People were unprepared to feed themselves. You set your disciples to work. Set us to work in a world where many are unprepared for life. Many brothers and sisters in life lack adequate food, clothing, and living conditions.

Lord, in your mercy, **R/**

Christ Jesus our Lord, bless us that we may be a blessing to others. Take our ambitions aad acquisitions and use them to your glory for the benefit of all. Sensitize us so that your kingdom work may be done with sensitivity. Help us use every situation as an opportunity for faith at work.

Lord, in your mercy, **R/**

Proper 13 — July 31-August 6 *(Common)*
Pentecost 11 *(Lutheran)*
Ordinary Time 18 *(Roman Catholic)*

Christ Jesus our Lord, direct the leaders of our land, church, and society. Use our abundance for your holy purpose.

Lord, in your mercy, **R/**

[Local and other specific prayer concerns:]

These and all other prayers which you would have us offer, we now bring, Father, before your throne of grace. Amen

Proper 14 — August 7-13 *(Common)*
Pentecost 12 *(Lutheran)*
Ordinary Time 19 *(Roman Catholic)*

ALMIGHTY GOD OF EARTH AND SEA, mountain and molecule, author of life and source of life. We praise and bless you.

Lord, in your mercy, **R**/

Lord, our lives are propelled into the unknown. Sometimes the obstacles of life discourage us, the struggles depress us, fears overcome us, and faith falters.

Lord, in your mercy, **R**/

Lord, you speak, "Take heart, it is I." Enable us to hear your voice, to rejoice in your presence, to give thanks, and worship you. Strengthen us for service.

Lord, in your mercy, **R**/

Son of God, we thank you for your gift of faith. We allow fear and doubt to dilute our faith. Fill us with faith equal to every demand and temptation. Compel us to your way.

Lord, in your mercy, **R**/

Proper 14 – August 7-13 *(Common)*
Pentecost 12 *(Lutheran)*
Ordinary Time 19 *(Roman Catholic)*

Son of God, we give thanks for vacation time, peace in our land, health, home, and happiness. Where these do not exist, we pray your hand of healing. Set us to accomplish your will for every life, beginning with ourselves.

Lord, in your mercy, **R**/

Son of God, you bid us "come." Equip us for service. Secure us for every insecure venture. Enable us to work together and support each other.

Lord, in your mercy, **R**/

[Local and other specific prayer concerns:]

These and all other prayers which you would have us offer, we now bring, Father, before your throne of grace. Amen

Proper 15 — August 14-20 *(Common)*
Pentecost 13 *(Lutheran)*
Ordinary Time 20 *(Roman Catholic)*

FATHER, SON, AND HOLY SPIRIT, we praise you. You are Lord, Word made flesh, comforter in life.

*Lord, in your mercy, **R**/*

O Lord, Son of David, we plead for help, guidance, strength, and faith. Grant us the confidence of the Canaanite woman, that persistence and faith, that untiring love for another. May knowing you as Father encourage us to be cheerful and forthright in our prayers and lives.

*Lord, in your mercy, **R**/*

O Lord, Savior, Redeemer, grant patience to all who call upon you. Forgive our impatience, our lack of faith in your wisdom and power. Fill us with desire to care about the well-being of others. Strengthen the faith of all who wait for prayers to be answered. Help us witness to your power with humility and commitment.

*Lord, in your mercy, **R**/*

O Lord, we are part of your body, the church. Guide us as a congregation. Prod us to reach out to others. Replace apathy with empathy. Help us to be supportive without being manipulative. Guide us as we move to autumn and busier lives. Guide and protect leaders of church and state. May you be able to say of us "Great is your faith."

*Lord, in your mercy, **R**/*

Proper 15 — August 14-20 *(Common)*
Pentecost 13 *(Lutheran)*
Ordinary Time 20 *(Roman Catholic)*

[Local and other specific prayer concerns:]

These and all other prayers which you would have us offer, we now bring, Father, before your throne of grace. Amen

Proper 16 — August 21-27 *(Common)*
Pentecost 14 *(Lutheran)*
Ordinary Time 21 *(Roman Catholic)*

GOD OF OUR ANCESTORS, of prophets, and people of faith. We praise you for your power, presence, trust, and love. You are our only God.

Lord, in your mercy, **R/**

Son of Man, who are you? You are always with us. You accept us when we are foolish. You love us when we are hateful. You cleanse us and forgive the sins we confess.

Lord, in your mercy, **R/**

Son of the Living God, your way is the way of humility. Your Word is the Word of love. Your will is the will for peace. All authority, power, and responsibility come from you. Guide us to maturity of judgment, sensitivity, and charity.

Lord, in your mercy, **R/**

Spirit of God, reveal yourself to your people. Build your church. Work in us to accomplish your will. We pray for those who suffer physical pain . . . We pray for all skeptics, cynics, agnostics, and atheists . . . We pray for all who suffer emotional distress.

Lord, in your mercy, **R/**

Proper 16 — August 21-27 *(Common)*
Pentecost 14 *(Lutheran)*
Ordinary Time 21 *(Roman Catholic)*

Bless us, Lord, to serve you always and only. Fill us with the comfort of your Good News and the courage of your love.

Lord, in your mercy, **R/**

[Local and other specific prayer concerns:]

These and all other prayers which you would have us offer, we now bring, Father, before your throne of grace. Amen

Proper 17 — August 28-September 3 *(Common)*
Pentecost 15 *(Lutheran)*
Ordinary Time 22 *(Roman Catholic)*

ALL WISE GOD, we worship you with thankful hearts. We are indebted for your mercy and grace. Your way is truth, our way is foolishness.

Lord, in your mercy, **R**/

Jesus, Lord, forgive us for condemning Peter but not criticizing ourselves. Forgive us when we accept Peter's way and reject your way. Forgive us when we allow Satan to use us to deny you.

Lord, in your mercy, **R**/

Jesus, our cross-bearer, show us your way of self-sacrifice. Plant your unmistaken logic in us, your clear purpose. Convince us that only desiring profit and gain is unworthy of the Christian life.

Lord, in your mercy, **R**/

Suffering Savior, enable us to give up our lives to accomplish your will: to visit the sick and imprisoned, to shelter the homeless, befriend the lonely and rejected, care for all in need, and announce your Word to all the world.

Lord, in your mercy, **R**/

Proper 17 — August 28-September 3 *(Common)*
Pentecost 15 *(Lutheran)*
Ordinary Time 22 *(Roman Catholic)*

We thank you, Lord, for prayers answered. Guide the leaders of church and state in the discharge of their duties. May we thirst for justice, and be filled with uncontrollable love that your will be done. Move us, Master, toward willing self-denial.

Lord, in your mercy, **R/**

[Local and other specific prayer concerns:]

These and all other prayers which you would have us offer, we now bring, Father, before your throne of grace. Amen

Proper 18 — September 4-10 *(Common)*
Pentecost 16 *(Lutheran)*
Ordinary Time 23 *(Roman Catholic)*

HEAVENLY FATHER, loving, caring Lord, you are with us in the struggle of daily life. We praise you.

Lord, in your mercy, **R**/

Christ, our brother, we use your name to curse; we live lives which discredit you. Forgive us for not seriously working at reconciliation. Forgive us for wanting to leave things as they are.

Lord, in your mercy, **R**/

Christ, our master, work through us as a family of faith. May we be able to trust one another, support one another, forgive one another as you love and forgive us.

Lord, in your mercy, **R**/

Christ, our Savior, we pray for all who minister as counselors, listening and responding to the hurt of suffering people. Teach us your way, O Lord. Bless us with patience and charity.

Lord, in your mercy, **R**/

Proper 18 — September 4-10 *(Common)*
Pentecost 16 *(Lutheran)*
Ordinary Time 23 *(Roman Catholic)*

Christ, our Redeemer, we pray for all who have sinned against us, made us angry, betrayed us. You forgive our sinful behavior, thoughtless words, and cruelty. Forgive our impatience, unfair criticism, and self-righteous attitudes.

Lord, in your mercy, **R**/

Christ in our midst, we pray for all in positions of authority. Protect them from harm and grant them wisdom. Grant that we be worthy subjects and bring honor to the Christ we name Lord.

Lord, in your mercy, **R**/

[Local and other specific prayer concerns:]

These and all other prayers which you would have us offer, we now bring, Father, before your throne of grace. Amen

Proper 19 — September 11-17 *(Common)*
Pentecost 17 *(Lutheran)*
Ordinary Time 24 *(Roman Catholic)*

KING OF THE KINGDOM OF HEAVEN, Lord of life, Messiah, Emmanuel, we offer prayers of praise and thanksgiving.

> *Lord, in your mercy,* **R/**

Master, we are indebted to you:
> you have welcomed us in baptism;
> you feed us in holy communion;
> you forgive all our sins through your love in Jesus Christ.

> *Lord, in your mercy,* **R/**

Master, direct our lives in every way:
> to love others as you love us;
> to forgive others as you forgive us;
> to serve others with your compassion and humility.

> *Lord, in your mercy,* **R/**

Merciful Master, we give thanks for life, love, health, and peace. Forgive us when we downgrade these blessings. We pray for all whose lives are filled with pain, fear, and adversity. We pray for our brothers and sisters at home and in every part of the world.

> *Lord, in your mercy,* **R/**

Proper 19 — September 11-17 *(Common)*
Pentecost 17 *(Lutheran)*
Ordinary Time 24 *(Roman Catholic)*

Forgiving Lord, open our minds to all you forgive in our lives. Remove complacency and denial. Guide leaders of church and state that they govern with compassion and wisdom. Grant hope to the troubled,
trust to the fearful,
faith to the fallen.
Lord, help us see that forgiveness is not counted, but lived.

Lord, in your mercy, **R**/

[Local and other specific prayer concerns:]

These and all other prayers which you would have us offer, we now bring, Father, before your throne of grace. Amen

Proper 20 — September 18-24 *(Common)*
Pentecost 18 *(Lutheran)*
Ordinary Time 25 *(Roman Catholic)*

GOD OF LOVE, we praise you for your generosity and commitment to your people. We praise you for the abundance of your grace.

*Lord, in your mercy, **R**/*

Lord of laborers, some have pleasant tasks, others demeaning chores; some are rewarded with affluence, others with rejection; some enjoy security, others uncertainty. Your love is for all. Lord, we are numbered among the laborers.

*Lord, in your mercy, **R**/*

Lord of life, fill us with joyful enthusiasm for the successful.
Enable us to compliment and congratulate with sincerity. Remove jealousy, rivalry, and hatred from our lives. Fill us with joyful satisfaction in your loving presence.

*Lord, in your mercy, **R**/*

Generous, loving Lord, we pray for all whose time and opportunities are running out. We pray for the destitute and discouraged. Grant hope and faith to the demoralized. Fill us with kindness and caring. Enable us to express your love and grace through our lives.

*Lord, in your mercy, **R**/*

Proper 20 — September 18-24 *(Common)*
Pentecost 18 *(Lutheran)*
Ordinary Time 25 *(Roman Catholic)*

O Lord, we raise before you those known to us who have special needs . . . We thank you, Lord, for prayers answered . . . May this coming week find us grateful, willing kingdom workers.

Lord, in your mercy, **R**/

[Local and other specific prayer concerns:]

These and all other prayers which you would have us offer, we now bring, Father, before your throne of grace. Amen

Proper 21 — September 25-October 1 (Common)
Pentecost 19 (Lutheran)
Ordinary Time 26 (Roman Catholic)

LORD GOD, Master of the vineyard of life, we praise you for your grace, for the gift of faith and love.

Lord, in your mercy, **R/**

Master, you ask that we work in your vineyard. Forgive our negative response, constant refusal, and continued excuses. Forgive us for time and energy spent doing selfish things.

Lord, in your mercy, **R/**

Master, you ask that we work in your vineyard. Forgive us when we say yes too easily and too quickly. O Lord, how successful your kingdom work would be if all who said yes meant it.

Lord, in your mercy, **R/**

Master, remove pride and conceit from our lives. Help us sincerely welcome the repentant person, whoever the person may be, whatever the person may have done. We are brothers and sisters in your grace.

Lord, in your mercy, **R/**

Proper 21 — September 25-October 1
(Common)
Pentecost 19 (Lutheran)
Ordinary Time 26 (Roman Catholic)

Master, fill us to overflowing with your Spirit, love, and joy. Be with all who are troubled, sick, and fearful. May the past not cloud your challenge to us in the present, nor our performance in the future.

Lord, in your mercy, **R**/

Master, we are your daughters and sons. You set us to work in a demanding harvest. Fill us with the power of your purpose and the intent of your love.

Lord, in your mercy, **R**/

[Local and other specific prayer concerns:]

These and all other prayers which you would have us offer, we now bring, Father, before your throne of grace. Amen

Proper 22 — October 2-8 *(Common)*
Pentecost 20 *(Lutheran)*
Ordinary Time 27 *(Roman Catholic)*

ALMIGHTY GOD, patient in love, abundant in mercy. Create in us clean hearts and right spirits. We praise you for your trusting love.

Lord, in your mercy, **R/**

Lord, our householder, you entrust to us a vineyard of beauty and promise.
> Forgive our carelessness.
> Remedy our destructiveness.
> Grant us the desire to protect your creation and the will to oversee it.

Lord, in your mercy, **R/**

Master of tenants, show us your way of humble obedience.
> Spare us from the foolishness of selfishness.
> Overcome us with desire for your will and way.
> Replace our autocratic behavior with meekness and mercy.

Lord, in your mercy, **R/**

Proper 22 — October 2-8 *(Common)*
Pentecost 20 *(Lutheran)*
Ordinary Time 27 *(Roman Catholic)*

Savior of the sinful, you know our devious nature. For-give our attempts to abuse and overcome. Overwhelm us with the might of your love and the power of your grace.

Lord, in your mercy, **R/**

Lord, our cornerstone, we pray for ourselves and our sinful nature. We pray for those whose lives touch ours and who tolerate us. We pray for those whom we name before you . . . We pray for leaders of church and state, remembering before you those who lead and guide our community . . . Create in us clean hearts and right spirits.

Lord, in your mercy, **R/**

[Local and other specific prayer concerns:]

These and all other prayers which you would have us offer, we now bring, Father, before your throne of grace. Amen

Proper 23 — October 9-15 *(Common)*
Pentecost 21 *(Lutheran)*
Ordinary Time 28 *(Roman Catholic)*

ALMIGHTY GOD OF PROPHET AND PARABLE, we gather to praise you for your love, goodness, and mercy. So infuse us with your will that we worship and serve you alone.

Lord, in your mercy, **R/**

Master of the marriage feast of life.
    You offer the abundance of creation.
    You prepare a place for us.
    Too often we reject your invitation and retaliate with
        ignorant independence.

Lord, in your mercy, **R/**

Almighty Host, remind us that you are King. Forgive us when we become offensive; chastise us for faithlessness and condescending conduct.
    Clothe us with correct apparel.
    Nurture us with humble pride.

Lord, in your mercy, **R/**

Proper 23 — October 9-15 *(Common)*
Pentecost 21 *(Lutheran)*
Ordinary Time 28 *(Roman Catholic)*

Spirit of God, move among your people, beginning with us.

Erase excusemaking and troublemaking from every agenda.

Fill us with tolerance and acceptance for all you invite to the feast of life.

Help us establish right priorities.

Lord, in your mercy, **R/**

Friend of sinners, not all who call you Lord are sincere. Forgive us when we allow familiarity to lead to disrespect. Hold before us the reality of our sin and the gift of your grace.

Lord, in your mercy, **R/**

[Local and other specific prayer concerns:]

These and all other prayers which you would have us offer, we now bring, Father, before your throne of grace. Amen

Proper 24 — October 16-22 *(Common)*
Pentecost 22 *(Lutheran)*
Ordinary Time 29 *(Roman Catholic)*

GOD OF TRUTH, Lord of lords, King of kings, we praise you. You give responsibility and freedom, grace and forgiveness. You are Lord.

Lord, in your mercy, **R**/

Teacher, you teach by example. Your way is truth. You care for every person in every circumstance.
   Grant us the will to follow your way.
   Plant patience in us that kindness and compassion
      blossom.
   Grant wisdom to cope with those who would trick
      and trap us.

Lord, in your mercy, **R**/

Lord Jesus, help us deal with life's puzzling options. Grant wisdom to know your best way. Too often we neither care for Caesar nor God. Separate us from selfishness. Attach us to your divine selflessness.

Lord, in your mercy, **R**/

Proper 24 — October 16-22 *(Common)*
Pentecost 22 *(Lutheran)*
Ordinary Time 29 *(Roman Catholic)*

Almighty God, grant to each the gift of discernment —
the ability to discern the divine from the material;
the ability to see the potential for good in all of life;
the ability to weigh your demands against those of
the world.
Enable us to render love that is genuine to both our
neighbor and to you, O Lord.

*Lord, in your mercy, **R**/*

Almighty God, guide the Caesars of this world. Protect them from harm. Cause them to use their power for the benefit of the poor in mind, body, and spirit.

*Lord, in your mercy, **R**/*

[Local and other specific prayer concerns:]

These and all other prayers which you would have us offer, we now bring, Father, before your throne of grace.
Amen

Proper 25 — October 23-29 *(Common)*
Pentecost 23 *(Lutheran)*
Ordinary Time 30 *(Roman Catholic)*

ALMIGHTY GOD, the commandments are yours; life is yours; we are yours. We gather to worship and praise you with hymns, prayers, and offerings.

Lord, in your mercy, **R/**

Almighty God, giver of commandments, author and source of love:
> focus our attention on your will to love;
> grant us the ability to love without anticipating reward;
> plant in us the desire to love that which we cannot understand.

Lord, in your mercy, **R/**

Almighty God, giver of every good thing. We thank you for the richness of your blessings. We thank you for the privilege of sharing what you have first given us. We thank you for all that we enjoy today, and for the part we can play in accomplishing your will. May we work together with enthusiasm and a positive attitude to fulfill your will.

Lord, in your mercy, **R/**

Proper 25 — October 23-29 *(Common)*
Pentecost 23 *(Lutheran)*
Ordinary Time 30 *(Roman Catholic)*

Almighty God, we remember before you friends who are ill . . . those who are troubled in mind, broken in spirit . . . We remember parents and children . . . all who are experiencing marital unhappiness . . . O Lord, we pray for the neighbor we know and appreciate, and for the neighbor we cannot understand and for whom we feel dislike . . .

Lord, in your mercy, **R/**

Almighty God, your commandment is simple. Prevent us from confusing the issue and shirking responsibility.

Lord, in your mercy, **R/**

[Local and other specific prayer concerns:]

These and all other prayers which you would have us offer, we now bring, Father, before your throne of grace. Amen

Proper 26 — October 30-November 5 *(Common)*
Pentecost 24 *(Lutheran)*
Ordinary Time 31 *(Roman Catholic)*

ALMIGHTY GOD OF PROPHET AND PARABLE,
Lord of lowly and Lord of lords. All honor and blessing
are yours.

Lord, in your mercy, **R**/

Lord our light, overcome our procrastination. Fill us
with desire to attend to the opportunity of the moment.
Fortify us with purpose and intent to fulfill your will.

Lord, in your mercy, **R**/

God of prayer, praise, and thanksgiving, you caution
us about pompous praise, lightweight loyalty, and care-
less celebration. Plant in us the desire for sincerity,
charity, and integrity.

Lord, in your mercy, **R**/

King of the kingdom of heaven, rule the lives of your
people. Keep before us the word of your commandments, the will of your grace. Give courage to the weak,
peace to the troubled, and hope to the loveless.

Lord, in your mercy, **R**/

Proper 26 — October 30-November 5 *(Common)*
Pentecost 24 *(Lutheran)*
Ordinary Time 31 *(Roman Catholic)*

Jesus our teacher, Jesus our master, lead us in your way of truth. Distraction comes easily. We allow weakness to lead us astray. May the road we take not lead to ruin, but return us to your grace.

Lord, in your mercy, **R**/

Jesus, our only master, prepare us for the demands of a new week. Focus our attention on your goal and will. Be with all for whom the coming week will be difficult and painful. We would bring your Good News and love.

Lord, in your mercy, **R**/

[Local and other specific prayer concerns:]

These and all other prayers which you would have us offer, we now bring, Father, before your throne of grace. Amen

Reformation Sunday (*Lutheran*)

LORD OF HOSTS, author of the way, the truth, and the life, blessing, honor, glory, and might be yours forever.

Lord, in your mercy, **R/**

Lord Jesus, praise you for your freedom work. Enable us to feel free, to be free, to give up all that would trap and hinder.
    Help us overcome overindulgence.
    Cause us to shed self-pity and pride.
    Dissuade us from relying on the faith of others.
    Grant faith able to move mountains of hopelessness
        and discouragement.

Lord, in your mercy, **R/**

Lord Jesus, we pray that we continue in your Word:
    no matter what the circumstance of daily life,
    no matter what the prospect for the future,
    no matter what the memory of the past.
Free all, Lord, who are trapped by sickness, who despair of life, who fear what is real and imaginary. Lift us out of our prisons and grant your freeing peace.

Lord, in your mercy, **R/**

Reformation Sunday *(Lutheran)*

Spirit of God, move among us. Remove apathy, lethargy. Fuel us with patience, caring, faith, and love. You have made us free. We praise you, Christ Jesus, our liberator.

Lord, in your mercy, **R/**

[Local and other specific prayer concerns:]

These and all other prayers which you would have us offer, we now bring, Father, before your throne of grace. Amen

All Saints' Sunday (*Common, Lutheran*)

ALMIGHTY GOD, your Word is made flesh among us in the mourning, the merciful, and meek. We praise you for coming to us and remaining with us.

Lord, in your mercy, **R**/

God of mercy and peace, you are with us in time of trouble and triumph. Help us see beyond ourselves to those who struggle beside us. Motivate us for peacemaking, for sharing our riches with the impoverished, our faith with the discouraged.

Lord, in your mercy, **R**/

Blessed Lord, many of us have neither been reviled nor persecuted. We are blessed with the freedom to worship. We are blessed with the opportunity to serve. Guide us in all we do.

Lord, in your mercy, **R**/

Spirit of God, we thank you for all who have helped us become who we are. We thank you for every faithful worker in your kingdom. We especially remember in our hearts those who are dear to us . . . So fill us with your Spirit that no false accusation or earthly want will ever be able to destroy your gift of faith.

Lord, in your mercy, **R**/

All Saints' Sunday *(Common, Lutheran)*

Thank you Lord, for every blessing. Bless your people with faith, hope, and love. Guide leaders of church and state in your way to blessedness.

Lord, in your mercy, **R/**

[Local and other specific prayer concerns:]

These and all other prayers which you would have us offer, we now bring, Father, before your throne of grace. Amen

Proper 27 — November 6-12 *(Common)*
Pentecost 25 *(Lutheran)*
Ordinary Time 32 *(Roman Catholic)*

ALMIGHTY MASTER AND CREATOR, you alone are
Lord. We praise you for your redeeming love and saving grace.

Lord, in your mercy, **R**/

Lord of every day and every occasion. Grant insight and
integrity to accomplish your will, wisdom to achieve
your goal, trust to serve without fear and fortified with
faith.

Lord, in your mercy, **R**/

God of love, not only does your peace pass all human
understanding, but so does your love and mercy. Enable us to love and forgive others as you love and forgive us.

Lord, in your mercy, **R**/

Lord, you grant life to us and place life before us;
    grant also the ability to establish right priorities;
    grant faithful perseverance to complete life's
       assignments;
    grant wisdom to invest time wisely and the talent
      you have entrusted to us.

Lord, in your mercy, **R**/

Proper 27 — November 6-12 *(Common)*
Pentecost 25 *(Lutheran)*
Ordinary Time 32 *(Roman Catholic)*

Lord, we praise you for every opportunity you allow. Guide leaders of church and state and those whom they serve. May you say of us, "Well done, good and faithful servant."

*Lord, in your mercy, **R/***

[Local and other specific prayer concerns:]

These and all other prayers which you would have us offer, we now bring, Father, before your throne of grace. Amen

Proper 28 — November 13-19 *(Common)*
Pentecost 26 *(Lutheran)*
Ordinary Time 33 *(Roman Catholic)*

HEAVENLY FATHER, Master, Teacher, all glory, power, and dominion are yours. We praise and worship you, the one true God.

Lord, in your mercy, **R**/

Lord, we praise you for the trust you place in us. We pray your guidance in the exercise of our tasks.
Spare us from jealousy and rivalry.
Detract us from foolish thought and behavior.
Move us into creative trust and fearless service.

Lord, in your mercy, **R**/

Lord, we praise you for every opportunity to worship you.
Grant us the gifts of certainty and sincerity.
Enable us to separate trimmings from truth, and ritual from righteousness.
Enable us to use the talent of praise with all our being.

Lord, in your mercy, **R**/

Proper 28 — November 13-19 *(Common)*
Pentecost 26 *(Lutheran*
Ordinary Time 33 *(Roman Catholic)*

Lord, help us practice what we preach.
>Plant in us faith which overcomes fear of the unknown.
>Fill us with trust in your Word to be able to cope with failure.
>Prevent us from succumbing to the curse of caution.
>Enable us to live by faith and with trust.
Your grace is sufficient for every fear and failure.

Lord, in your mercy, **R/**

[Local and other specific prayer concerns:]

These and all other prayers which you would have us offer, we now bring, Father, before your throne of grace. Amen

136

Pentecost 27 *(Lutheran only)*

CREATOR GOD, living Spirit, we gather to worship and praise you, the only God. We praise you for your goodness, mercy, and steadfast love.

*Lord, in your mercy, **R/***

Christ Jesus, we question the present and fear the future. Prophets make their predictions and we are filled with fear and uncertainty. Fill us with the certainty that you are always with us.

*Lord, in your mercy, **R/***

Christ Jesus, help us discern the false from the true. Keep us from being led astray. It is easy to become alarmed by daily events and to question your power. Fill us with good thoughts, faith, hope, and love.

*Lord, in your mercy, **R/***

Christ Jesus, we pray for all who are being led astray. We pray for those who are misleading others. May your Word overcome every evil intent. Help us see our weaknesses and vulnerability. Strengthen us for service. May our lives be an expression of commitment in you, O Lord.

*Lord, in your mercy, **R/***

Pentecost 27 *(Lutheran only)*

Christ Jesus, with the Father since the beginning. May wars and rumors of war, terrible times, and fearful occurrences increase our faith in you. Use our faith to support and sustain those in difficult times.

Lord, in your mercy, **R**/

[Local and other specific prayer concerns:]

These and all other prayers which you would have us offer, we now bring, Father, before your throne of grace. Amen

Proper 29 — November 20-26 *(Common)*
Christ The King
Ordinary Time 34 *(Roman Catholic)*

ALMIGHTY GOD, Blessed Father, Creator of diversity. We gather to worship you with our days, means, and talents.

Lord, in your mercy, **R**/

Son of Man, you are with us in the routine of daily life:
   you see us in every place in the world;
   you see us in every strata of society;
   you see us in every kind of need.
Open our eyes to the needs of others. Open our hearts to service and love.

Lord, in your mercy, **R**/

Son of Man, the daily news reminds us of global needs. Often we feel helpless. Sometimes we do not care. We can do so little and the need is so great. Work your miracle in the little we are able to do. Remove every feeling of helplessness and despair. Fill us with love and determination.

Lord, in your mercy, **R**/

Proper 29 — November 20-26 *(Common)*
Christ The King
Ordinary Time 34 *(Roman Catholic)*

Son of Man, work your miracles through your people. Find us willing conduits for your compassion and love. We remember before you the starving and sick . . . We remember the discouraged and dying . . . We remember the healthy and wealthy who lack purpose in life . . .

Lord, in your mercy, **R/**

Christ the King, all honor and glory are yours. We serve you by serving others. We praise you by responding to the cries and crises of others. You are Lord; you are King. You are our Redeemer and Savior.

Lord, in your mercy, **R/**

[Local and other specific prayer concerns:]

These and all other prayers which you would have us offer, we now bring, Father, before your throne of grace. Amen

www.ingramcontent.com/pod-product-compliance
Lightning Source LLC
Chambersburg PA
CBHW052108090426
42741CB00009B/1722